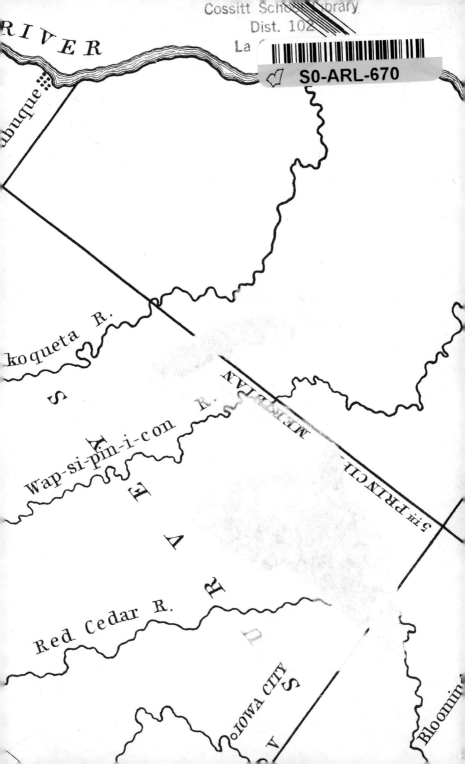

"I wanted the children now to understand more about the beginnings of things. . .to know what is behind the things they see. . .what it is that made America as they know it."

LAURA INGALLS
WILDER

PIONEER AND AUTHOR

☐

by William Anderson

Foreword by Professor Ruth Alexander

☐

The Kipling Press • New York

Foreword

□

Laura Ingalls Wilder was only one of many writers who found homesteading on the American prairie over a hundred years ago an exciting subject to write about. In fact, her work was not taken as seriously as better-known writers of the Middle West such as Willa Cather, Ole Rolvaag, and Hamlin Garland. Literary scholars and critics paid almost no attention to her writing until millions of children who had loved her stories persuaded them to recognize the "Little House" books as American children's classics.

Now, some thirty years after Laura's death, her writing is greatly admired. She captures in words the sights, sounds, and feeling of living on the prairie, and the warm affection of a loving, courageous family. Her books have furnished, in a greatly altered version, the basis for a television series. Loyal fans have made museums of her last home at Mansfield, Missouri, and the "surveyors' house" in DeSmet, South Dakota, where Laura lived on the open prairie.

Laura grew up in the last three decades of the nineteenth century. She was part of the climax of the great westward movement which had settled the American continent. What began as slow trickles of people west out of the first settlements in Virginia, Massachusetts, New York, and Florida in the 1600's, became a mighty flood after the Civil War.

Most of the pioneers wanted land to farm. Whole families packed their belongings in covered wagons drawn by ox teams and moved west to seek a new life. Thousands of Norwegian, Swedish, German, and Slavic people sailed across the Atlantic, came as far west as possible by train, and joined the Americans in their westward trek. They faced backbreaking work and physical hardships before they could build homes and create towns. They encountered blizzards, tornadoes, grasshoppers, deer, antelope, buffalo, grizzly bears, sometimes hostile Indians who regarded them as intruders, and miles and miles of open plains and prairie.

Laura's family was part of this dramatic migration. Her books trace her life—from her earliest memories in Wisconsin where she was born (*Little House in the Big Woods*, 1932) to her first job as a country school teacher and her marriage to Almanzo Wilder (*These Happy Golden Years*, 1943). In between, the tales relate the family's homesteading adventure in Kansas (*On the Banks of Plum Creek*, 1937), and finally homesteading in Dakota Territory (*By the Shores of Silver Lake*, 1939; *The Long Winter*, 1940, and *Little Town on the Prairie*, 1941). Another book told of Almanzo's boyhood on a New York farm (*Farmer Boy*, 1933), and after Laura's death in 1957, a volume recounting the early years of her marriage (*The First Four Years*, 1971) was published.

Laura Ingalls Wilder lived at the same time as Mark Twain and Rudyard Kipling, yet she was not a famous writer at that time. She did not even begin writing her books until she was over sixty years old. After she and Almanzo moved to Missouri, she became a successful chicken farmer and wrote occasional articles for farm journals. Her daughter, Rose Wilder Lane, already a newspaper journalist, encouraged her mother to write down the stories she had loved as a child. She also helped her publish them.

The stories are primarily happy memories of Laura's childhood. She overlooks and omits some of the tragedies that accompanied much homesteading. For her, the prairie was wild and beautiful. She describes the wild flowers as she explored the prairie with her blind sister, Mary. She tells of riding a friend's horse across the open country. She watched the railroads being built. She stared down a wolf one silent, snowy, moonlit night. Yet Laura does not sentimentalize the hardships that she does recount: grinding wheat in a coffee grinder to make bread; burning prairie hay to keep warm; living with a fear-crazed and violent woman while she taught country school. In Laura's world, such troubles could be met and overcome in a loving family by hard work, cooperation, and patience.

Laura makes an adventure out of daily life—helping Ma make a green tomato pie, cleaning ticks from her straw bed, building furniture, singing to Pa's fiddle on long winter evenings. These events, so closely related to our own experience, are recreated in vivid detail. She makes the domestic side of pioneering exciting, using rich materials ignored by those male writers and historians who have concentrated on the heroic actions of fighting Indians and taming the wilderness.

While Laura is the heroine in these stories, readers become acquainted with the whole Ingalls family through her eyes. However simple and plain their home, the Ingalls remain a stable, caring family. Ma holds them together through their many moves and teaches Laura to clean, cook, and sew (essential skills in pioneer life). Pa is her cherished companion outdoors, where Laura prefers to be, and he enchants the family with his fiddle playing. Her sisters—blind Mary, for whom she "sees", playmate Carrie, and baby Grace—keep the narrative lively and believable. Depictions of numerous friends and relatives still ring true today.

At the end of this multi-volume saga, Laura is an independent young woman starting a family of her own. Laura Ingalls Wilder combined the story of a young girl's maturation with the story of America's westward movement. Her treatment of the material is sometimes superficial and she ignores the grimmer, more painful side of pioneering—dirt, failure, misery, violence, destruction of land and Indian culture. Nonetheless, she has written clearly and movingly of a great epoch in American history from the viewpoint of a woman remembering her childhood. Children's literature is immeasurably richer from her work.

—*Ruth Alexander*
  South Dakota State University
  September 28, 1986

LAURA INGALLS WILDER

Pioneer and Author

Charles and Caroline (Pa and Ma) Ingalls.

Pioneer Family

□

*"In those days, once
people started going
west they usually
kept on."*

During the Civil War, the American government
passed a law that had no connection with the fighting which
had separated the North and the South. When President
Lincoln signed his name to a document which created the
Homestead Act of 1862, an exciting opportunity became
available to each American. It was the chance to claim open
lands belonging to the United States government, especially
in the areas which comprised the American West.

Beyond the Mississippi River, all the way to the Pacific
coastline, lay millions of acres of unsettled land. Some of the
tracts were called the Great American Desert and were
thought to be too dry and unfit for farming, but much of the
area west of the Mississippi was prairie land, covered by miles

of waving grass. Few trees grew there, but the soil was fertile and black and open for settlement.

Each American citizen over the age of twenty-one was eligible to file a claim for the government's homestead land. The open plains had been surveyed and divided into squares of 160 acres each, which on maps looked like a mammoth checkerboard. In the 1860's, most of that land was lonely and unoccupied, waiting for settlers to arrive.

There were only a few requirements for filing land claims. The homesteader had to officially register his claim at a land office, where record keeping was done. A house must be built on the claim, and the prairie land plowed up to show that in the future a farm would exist. For six months each year, the homesteader or a family member must live on the property. Some homesteaders hired "claim-sitters" to protect their property from "claim-jumpers" and to fulfill the requirement.

At the end of five years, when all the government specifications were met, the land became the homesteader's property. The government issued a "patent" which meant that the homestead ownership passed from the United States to the man or woman who had developed it as a farm and home.

The Homestead Act was exciting news for many Americans. Where else would a government give a citizen land just for the asking? A happy song was sung, describing the Homestead Act:

Oh come to this country
And don't you feel alarm
For Uncle Sam is rich enough
To give us all a farm!

Europeans heard of the amazing offer of free land and immigrants sailed across the Atlantic Ocean to become American homesteaders. In America's Eastern towns, villages and crowded farming neighborhoods, people were lured by the stories of good hunting, level rich farmlands and the chance to pioneer in the American West.

When the Civil War ended in 1865, thousands of soldiers decided to head west to see what lay beyond the Great River, the Mississippi. The river somehow became a dividing line between east and west. "The Great River Road," as it was called, split America from north to south. From its headwaters in Minnesota to the port of New Orleans in the south, where it emptied into the Gulf of Mexico, the Mississippi was not only a north-south waterway, but also a crossroads for pioneers traveling west toward the sunset.

Just five years after the Homestead Act became a part of American history, a baby girl was born deep in the forest only seven miles from the Mississippi. Her entire life was shaped by the westward movement. She was Laura Ingalls Wilder. She first lived the life of a pioneer girl and then when the experience of the frontier was memory, wrote down her tales of growing up in the West. Her stories, known as the "Little House" books, have given the world a sharp, clear picture of life in the woods and on the plains during the last phase of American pioneering, from the 1860's to the 1890's. But when Laura Elizabeth Ingalls was born on February 7, 1867, in a log cabin near Pepin, Wisconsin, no one imagined the remarkable life she would live, first as a pioneer and then as a much-loved author.

The importance of Laura's work as the author of the "Little House" books is that she recorded a period of American life which historians call westward expansion. But during her experiences as a pioneer girl and then as a farmer's wife, Laura Ingalls Wilder was too busy living her life to write about it. Only after she was sixty did she think about writing of the pioneering people and adventures she remembered so well.

Laura explained that her desire to write was a feeling that what she had seen and experienced on the prairies were "stories that had to be told." She said that what she remembered of the pioneer days "was altogether too good to be lost."

As Laura realized that she had participated in an important phase of American life in the pioneering era, she felt surprised to think of the many changes she had seen in her own lifetime. "I wanted the children now to understand more about the beginnings of things," Laura said, "to know what is behind the things they see—what it is that made America as they know it. Then I thought of writing the story of my childhood in several volumes—an eight volume historical novel covering every aspect of the American frontier."

The job Laura planned to do—to write about the frontier—was one which kept historians researching and writing for years. But the history she wove into the "Little House" stories was close and familiar. Because she had lived it, Laura could describe life as a pioneer in a way that history books could not. "I understood that in my own life I represented a period of American history," she marvelled.

As a writer, Laura possessed what few authors do: enough personal adventure and impressions to write without research. "I had seen the whole frontier," Laura wrote, "the woods, the Indian country of the great plains, the frontier towns, the building of railroads in wild, unsettled country, homesteading and farmers coming in to take possession. I realized that I had seen and lived it all—all the successive phases of the frontier, first the frontiersman, then the pioneer, then the farmers, and the towns."

Through Laura's keen memories, her sharp vision and her storytelling skill, we can still experience the pioneer West as she saw it.

When Laura Ingalls was born in the Wisconsin woods, the land there was still raw and wild. The region was called "The Big Woods" because the forests stretched out for miles. Panthers and bears roamed through the brush, and the big trees nearly blotted out the sky overhead. Only the presence of farmers, trappers and hunters made the country seem more civilized. Pioneers settled on clearings in the woods surrounding Lake Pepin. In the winter, the men hunted and trapped furs to trade in the village of Pepin on the lakeshore. In the summer, they tended their gardens and planted fields on the cleared land. Wood for fuel and the building of log houses was everywhere.

Laura's parents were Wisconsin pioneers. In 1860, Charles Philip Ingalls married Caroline Lake Quiner, and they left their homes to journey north into the Wisconsin woods. "My parents possessed the spirit of the frontier to a marked degree," Laura explained. In her book *Little House in the Big Woods,* she described her family's life in their first home.

Charles Ingalls, who was always called Pa by his girls, was a jolly man. A trapper, a woodsman, a carpenter, a farmer and a merry fiddler, Pa was a shrewd frontiersman, meeting each hardship with spirit and skill. In the evenings, after long days working in his fields or tramping through the Big Woods on hunting trips, Pa entertained his family by playing his violin

and telling stories. He told Indian legends, family tales of adventure, and humorous versions of his own experiences. Pa's storytelling sessions in the firelit log cabin were always memorable. Laura never forgot Pa's stories, and it is easy to see where she acquired her own talent for telling a good tale.

From her mother, Laura learned to cherish books and create a homelike feeling wherever she went. Ma Ingalls was firm and capable; she was content to stay in one place while Pa was always eager to see new lands and seek new homes. "Mother was descended from an old Scotch family," Laura said, "and she inherited the Scotch thriftiness. Although born and raised on the frontier, Caroline Ingalls was an educated, cultured woman. She was very quiet and gentle, but proud and particular in all matters of "good breeding."

Together Pa and Ma Ingalls were a pioneer team, well suited to life on the frontier. Ma understood Pa's restless nature and his need to move on. And wherever they were, Ma could make a home, whether around a campfire miles from the nearest neighbor or in a moving covered wagon or a drafty claim shanty.

Plum Creek today.

To Plum Creek and Back Again

□

*"I can still plainly
see the grass and
the trees and the
path winding ahead,
flecked with sunshine..."*

Mary, Laura's older sister, was born in Pa and Ma's log cabin in the woods near Pepin in 1865. The little log house, her parents, and her sister were Laura's first memories. But by the late 1860's, the forest had started to disappear. The wagon trail in front of the Ingalls' cabin became a road. Farmers cleared away the woods, building houses and planting fields. Pa did not like these changes. He knew about the free land in the West and was eager to farm on the open, level lands. When a newcomer offered to buy the Ingalls' house and farm, Pa was eager to sell out and move West.

When Pa and Ma discussed moving, Ma looked around her snug house and at Mary and Laura, who were both under five, and wondered why they should leave. Ma had been a teacher, and as Pa said, she had a way with words. When she was a schoolgirl, she had written a composition in school about her feelings for home and family. "Who would wish to venture out away from home?" she had written, when there was warmth and security and loving faces nearby.

But Pa was determined to homestead in Kansas, where there was plenty of free land and fewer people than there were in the Big Woods.

Laura was just two when her parents packed up all they owned, loaded the covered wagon, and said good-bye to the family and friends who stayed behind in Wisconsin. Pa drove the horses through the Big Woods to the shores of Lake Pepin, which was actually a wide spot in the Mississippi River. The ice was still thick on the river, so it became the bridge from east to west as Pa and his girls crossed over it. On the other side was the state of Minnesota.

The long journey to Indian country in Kansas took the Ingalls family across Minnesota, Iowa, Missouri, and finally into Kansas. Laura tells of the trip in her book, *Little House on the Prairie*. Although she was too young to remember this journey with Pa and Ma and Mary, they told her about it later—of crossing dangerous rivers and streams, of losing

Jack, the family bulldog, and finding him again, of traveling miles and miles without seeing another human being.

When the Ingalls family reached southern Kansas, Pa finally saw a spot he liked. There was nothing but grass and level prairie land under the blue sky. But Pa knew they were not far from the Verdigris River, and Walnut Creek was nearby. The timber along the streams would provide wood for fuel and building on the treeless prairie. The pioneer town of Independence, Kansas was thirteen miles away, but as Pa said, it might as well be a hundred. Thirteen miles was a long journey with a team of horses and a loaded wagon.

Establishing a home on the prairie was a long process. Pa cut trees for a log cabin, hauled them to the building site and slowly raised the walls. Then he dug a well for water and built a barn for the horses. With his breaking plow, he changed grasslands into fields. Breaking the prairie was grunting hard labor. The tall grass country was not used to the steel edge of a plow cutting and turning the sod. Sometimes the grassroots were so thick that Pa had to attack them with his ax before the plow could pass through.

The land Pa chose for a homestead was actually Indian country. The Osage tribe had used it for its hunting grounds, and the Ingalls family often saw the Osages at a distance. One day, Pa took Laura and Mary on a long walk to one of their abandoned camps. It was August 3, 1870. Laura remembered the date well, because when she, Mary and Pa returned to the cabin, a baby sister awaited them. A neighbor lady was there with Ma. While Pa and the girls were away, Caroline Celestia Ingalls had been born. When Carrie's birth was recorded in the Ingalls' family Bible, the place was given as Montgomery County, Kansas.

It seemed as if Ingalls were settled on the land for good when the Osages grew disturbed that so many settlers were invading the homeland they had been promised by the American government. Pa Ingalls' cabin was three miles into what was called the Osage Diminished Reserve and a dim Indian trail ran by the house. "My childish memories hold the sound of the war-whoop and I see pictures of painted Indians," Laura said of her last memories of Kansas. Rumors spread among the neighbors who lived near the Ingalls that the United States cavalry would drive all the settlers away.

Pa declared that he would not wait to be driven off land he had settled on. Meanwhile, far away in the Big Woods, Gus Gustafson, the man who bought the Ingalls farm, could not pay for it. A letter arrived in Kansas saying that Pa and Ma could have their Wisconsin farm back. They decided to leave the prairies and return home.

When Pa and Ma filled the wagon with their belongings and stretched the white canvas overhead, Laura's first pioneering adventure was over. They were going home, to a place Laura hardly remembered.

When the Ingalls family settled back into the log cabin near Pepin, Laura began to see and notice the small things of life—the sights and sounds and smells that make up living. She began storing up images and sensations that many years later would make her a writer who could transport readers into a time and place long ago and far away. Many years later Laura wrote about this period in *Little House in the Big Woods*.

Laura's first discovery of books and reading came soon after the Wisconsin homecoming. A half-mile down the road from the Ingalls' cabin was the Barry Corner School, and Mary Ingalls was old enough to attend. Each morning she set out with her bright new dinner pail and her schoolbook. When she returned, she told Laura all about her day at school, and showed her how to read. Finally, the day came when Laura was old enough to trot along to school with her big sister. Their teacher, Annie Barry, helped awaken Laura's lifelong fascination with words.

When she was a famous writer, Laura was asked how she had become an author. "The only reason I can think of," She said, "is that Pa and Ma were great readers and I read a lot at home with them." Both Pa and Ma valued books.

On Laura's sixth birthday Pa bought her a book of verses called "The Floweret." It became one of her most treasured possessions. The Ingalls family was in Lake City, Minnesota that day, on the other side of Lake Pepin, because once again, they were moving west—this time to Minnesota where the land stretched out into the plains.

At six, Laura had already participated in two major moves west. While it might seem difficult to leave home to venture into unknown territories, to the American pioneer moving west was an adventure. Pioneers believed that "it is better, farther on," and that was how Laura's family felt. "Our needs were simple," Laura said. "It wasn't so hard to put all our possessions in one covered wagon. The important thing was that we had the family and our own strengths and pleasures. Pa could always play wonderful music on his fiddle and drive the cares away, and Ma read the Bible to give us courage."

Laura always remembered the journey across Minnesota. She wrote:

The grass along the road was fresh and green in the springtime sun and it was a delight to camp at night in little nooks along the way. Nearly always we stopped by a creek or a small river, where there was plenty of water and sticks to make a campfire. We'd see the sun go down, hear the birds twitter their sleepy goodnights and sleep with the horses crunching their oats in their feedbox at the back of the wagon with just the thin cover between their heads and ours.

One evening, Laura was jarred out of sleep by the sound of a long, clear train whistle. Railroads were stretching their tracks west, almost alongside the pioneers as they traveled. Close to the prairie track Pa used to guide the horses west was a new railroad line. Laura had never seen a train, and Ma told her to look quickly to see the engine and the cars speeding by. Laura remembered that:

I looked, and in the twilight saw the engine and a train, the first I had ever seen. I held my breath while it went by, the engine puffing and the wheels rattling on the iron rails. One of the cars had lighted windows, and through them I could see people, sitting, riding on through the dark. We were all silent, watching till the train was out of sight. Then Pa said we were living in a great age. He said that in a day a train covered more distance than an ox-team could travel in a week, and he spoke of railroads conquering the Great American Desert.

Laura, Mary, and Carrie (circa 1881)

A Prairie Home

□

> *"Golden years are*
> *passing by, Happy,*
> *happy golden years.*
> *Passing on the wings*
> *of time, These happy*
> *golden years."*

When the Ingalls family arrived at what Laura called "the prettiest place by the prettiest creek we had ever seen," they had arrived at the new homestead Pa hoped for. The stream was called Plum Creek. On its high bank was a dugout house, all ready for the Ingalls family to move in.

Two miles away from their new home was the village of Walnut Grove, Minnesota. Ma was glad to be near a town, as there would be a school and a church. And Pa was pleased because the Winona and St. Peter Railroad passed through Walnut Grove. The railroad had arrived in 1873, the year the Ingalls family came to Plum Creek. Pa planned to raise bumper wheat crops on his farm, and the railroad was necessary to ship away crops to the big flour mills in eastern Minnesota.

While Pa worked his land and Ma kept house, Mary and Laura went back to school. "We were just two wild Indians, seven and nine years old and on our own for the first time," Laura said of the day when she and Mary started at the Walnut Grove school. She and Mary studied in old schoolbooks that Ma gave them, and they shared a slate and pencil.

When Pa's wheat crop was a lush green in the field, the entire family had the feeling, Laura later said, that "it was a good world." They had moved away from the dugout; across the creek and nearer to Walnut Grove. There Pa built a house of sawn boards, with glass windows, factory-made doors and china doorknobs. In *On the Banks of Plum Creek*, Laura wrote about the excitment of "the wonderful house" and their adventures along the creek.

She described the terrible day when swarms of grasshoppers, in clouds huge enough to blot out the sun, descended on the prairie. Within minutes, the insects ate everything in sight. The Ingalls' wheat crop, their garden, and even the

plum thicket along the creek were all destroyed. Laura said that the Minnesota grasshopper invasion of 1874 was the worst since the ancient plagues of Egypt.

"I have lived among uncounted millions of grasshoppers," Laura wrote later. "I saw their bodies choke Plum Creek. I saw them destroy every green thing on the face of the earth." With his crops gone, Pa was forced to leave his girls and walk hundreds of miles from home to find work. He found a job as a harvester in the untouched wheatfields in eastern Minnesota, and returned in the fall when the work ended.

Grasshoppers were not the only hazard on the Minnesota prairie. In the winter a blizzard could come out of nowhere, bringing hours or days of fierce cold, wind and blinding snow. "The blizzards," Laura explained, "always came quick enough to catch people unprepared. No one measured the speed of the wind in those days, but surely it was as fast as a hurricane speed. Whichever way one went into a blizzard, he went against it." Pa was once lost in a blizzard, and spent days huddled in a sheltered mound of snow along Plum Creek's bank, while the family waited and worried just steps away in the warm house.

Pa was determined to raise a wheat crop on the Plum Creek farm. But in 1875 dry weather and grasshoppers ruined his fields again. He walked east once more, working for wages as a harvester. When he returned, winter was near, and Pa moved the family into Walnut Grove. It was too far to walk from the farm to town during the winter months. And although Ma was a good teacher herself, she insisted that the girls attend school whenever they could.

When the Ingalls family had settled in town, Laura returned home from school one day to find a new baby brother! The date was November 1, 1875 and the boy was named Charles Frederick.

Though Pa could work as a carpenter in Walnut Grove, he was still restless. The countryside was so infested with grasshoppers that he could not harvest his own grain before the 'hoppers ate it. He longed for new opportunities. Then, Mr. and Mrs. Steadman, friends from Walnut Grove, offered Pa and Ma the chance to help them run a hotel in eastern Iowa. The Masters Hotel in Burr Oak was a busy place, and there would be plenty of work there.

When difficulties in the West grew too great, pioneer families often returned to their homes. This was called "back-trailing," and that is what Pa Ingalls did by leaving Walnut Grove. Both he and Laura felt it keenly. "How I wished we were going west!" Laura admitted. "Pa did not like to turn his back on the West either."

The journey was difficult. The Ingalls' new baby, Freddie was not well. Pa and Ma and the girls stopped to visit relatives in South Troy, Minnesota. But the fun of seeing cousins and aunts and uncles was shadowed by the baby's illness. On August 27, 1876, Freddie suddenly died. Leaving his little grave behind was perhaps the harshest challenge the Ingalls family ever faced.

When Laura first saw Burr Oak, she noticed immediately that it was different from the fresh newness of Walnut Grove. Burr Oak, Laura said, was "an old town, built of red brick...I liked a new town better and I knew Pa did too." It was a quiet village, except for all the activity that centered on the Masters Hotel where Laura and her family would live.

The Ingalls family settled in for the winter, and soon Pa and Ma were absorbed in the hotel work. There were steady boarders, those who were passing through, and often dozens of covered wagons parked near the shelter of the hotel.

But the noise and the crowds of the hotel did not suit Pa and Ma. Soon they rented a brick house in Burr Oak and were living there when their last child was born. She was Grace, and was born on May 23, 1877.

The Ingalls family spent two years in Burr Oak, and Pa worked at a variety of jobs. But he longed to go west again. That was the peculiar trait of the pioneer, an endless fascination with the West. It was odd, Laura said, because "everything came at us out of the West...storms, blizzards, grasshoppers, burning hot winds and fires...yet it seemed that we wanted nothing so much as we wanted to keep on going west!" And so, it did not surprise their old friends in Walnut Grove when the Ingalls family moved back there in 1878. The Plum Creek land had been sold, so Pa built a house in town. Here, Pa worked as a carpenter, and served as justice of the peace. The girls also attended school regularly, which pleased Ma. It was a happy time for the Ingalls. There were church socials to go to and picnics in the big grove of walnut trees near town.

Then tragedy struck. In the spring of 1879, Mary Ingalls became ill with what was called "brain fever." She was sick for weeks. Ma and Pa feared she would die. At last she recovered, but she was left blind. On that sorrowful day, Pa solemnly gave Laura a duty. She was to become Mary's link to light and action by repeating what she saw of the world. Laura accepted her new role as Mary's eyes. She now saw twice, once for herself and again for her sister. In this way, Laura began to observe the world as a writer would.

Now Pa needed a job. There were doctor bills, charges to pay, and his growing family to feed, clothe and educate.

In 1879, the railroad was extended from Minnesota into the Dakota Territory. Everyone could talk of nothing else. When Pa was offered a job as timekeeper and paymaster in the railroad construction camps, he accepted eagerly. He couldn't wait to go west again and perhaps find more of Uncle Sam's free land for himself.

So the Ingalls family moved west once more to the Dakota Territory. It would be their last stop. Pa went ahead to handle paying the railroad men at the camps where they were building the tracks. Ma and the girls waited in Walnut Grove while Mary regained her strength. When they left town, they traveled by train. It was Laura's first trip on the railroad.

Laura and Pa in the Ingalls family portrait (1890's)

Pioneer Wife

□

| *"The only way to go*
is ahead." |

When the Ingalls family was reunited on the Dakota prairie, their first home was a tiny shanty set apart from the bunkhouses, stables, and cook houses of the Silver Lake camp. There were no towns in the Dakota Territory as yet. But the once silent prairies were now alive with the sounds of men and horses and building.

The men continued building the railroad into the late autumn when they returned to their homes in the East. Everyone left except the Ingalls family. The head surveyor at the Silver Lake camp offered Pa the use of the surveyors' house on the lakeshore. Pa and Ma agreed it would be a good opportunity, even though they would be miles from any neighbor. Early in the spring, the country would once again become busy with homesteaders. A town would be started. Pa learned that its name would be De Smet.

Laura wrote of the winter of 1879-1880 when her family lived alone on the Dakota prairie in *By the Shores of Silver Lake*. The days and evenings in the surveyor's house were cozy and pleasant. In the warmth of the coal fire, the girls knitted and sewed, told stories and played games. Often Pa was gone on long tramps across the snowy prairie, trapping and hunting and looking over the countryside. In the evenings, after their good meals made from the supplies left in the surveyor's pantry, Pa played his fiddle. Before the snow set in, Pa had bought a supply of books, newspapers, and magazines. These were read by the light of the kerosene lamp that glowed over the red-checkered tablecloth, as the icy wind whistled outside. Ma read aloud so blind Mary could enjoy the new stories. Pa located a choice homestead claim, just a mile from the town site. He filed on it at the land office in Brookings.

Winter had hardly ended before hoards of landseekers started arriving. A lighted lamp was kept in the window of the surveyors' house because it was the only shelter for miles around. Suddenly, Pa and Ma found themselves in the hotel business again. As many as twenty weary travelers crowded the floor of the house, rolled up in blankets. All of them were hungry and cold. They were glad to pay Ma 25¢ for a meal and 25¢ for a place to sleep. Ma's meals were simple but satisfying. Usually there was salt pork, crisply fried potatoes, baked beans, hot tea, and Ma's delicious sourdough biscuits. With no milk available, she made bread and biscuits from dough made from soured water and flour. When a homesteader asked her to write down her recipes, Ma exclaimed, "Goodness! I never measure anything!"

In April, 1880, buildings went up along Main Street, and business began immediately in the new town.

Pa bought two lots along Main Street for himself, and built store buildings on each site. As one of the first settlers, Pa Ingalls was important in the formation of the town of De Smet. He became justice of the peace and helped to start the Congregational Church.

But town life was not what the Ingalls family wanted. They preferred life on the farm. So they were happy when Pa quickly built a claim shanty on the homestead claim. It was a tiny house, certainly the smallest of all the "little houses." Ma laughed when she saw it, saying that "it looks like half a woodshed that has been split along the ridgepole!" But it became home, and surrounding the house site, Pa planted little cottonwood saplings brought from a nearby lake. There was a tree for each of his girls on the otherwise treeless land. And the cottonwoods Pa planted that spring day in 1880 still thrive.

Laura wished, as did Pa, that they could go further west, but her only journeys west were with Mary to the top of the low hill on the homestead to see the prairie sunsets. As the sun dropped in the sky and clouds were tinted with purple and gold and pink and red, Laura described the spectacle to her sister. "You make pictures when you talk, Laura," Mary would say.

Though the Ingalls family preferred life on the homestead, it was the town of De Smet which offered them refuge during the winter of 1880-1881. That was the infamous "Hard Winter." Blizzards blew for six months, and all sources of supply for the little community of one hundred people were shut down. After an October blizzard caught the Ingalls family unprepared in their drafty claim shanty, Pa moved them to his store building in town.

For a few weeks, Laura and Carrie attended De Smet's first school. But soon blizzards clogged the railroad tracks, ending school and stopping all traffic and supply trains. Coal became scarce, and stores grew empty. By Christmastime, the situation looked dismal. In January the railroad company announced that it was impossible to keep the tracks cleared. Service was suspended until spring.

In the tiny kitchen of Pa's building, the Ingalls family worked together to survive. Laura turned fourteen that

winter and she stoutly helped Pa and Ma in the daily battle for heat and food. When coal supplies were gone, the pioneers burned hay. Twisted into sticks, the hay made a hot, quick flame—but the supply had to be constantly replenished. Laura's hands grew raw and rough as she helped keep the fire going. The food stores were all eaten until wheat was the only supply left. The Ingalls family ground the grain in their coffee mill for a daily loaf of bread.

"There is something about living close to the great elemental forces of nature that allows people to rise above small annoyances and discomforts," Laura said of the Hard Winter. Everyone in De Smet survived, and finally when the snowdrifts melted in May, the clear, piercing sound of the train whistle was once again heard. Laura's account of her family's survival is told in *The Long Winter*.

In 1882, Mary went away to the Iowa College for the Blind. Pa and Ma managed to send her there for the entire seven-year course. Mary learned braille and raised print reading; she excelled in all her studies, especially literature and music. She also learned many crafts then taught to the blind, including beadwork, weaving and needlecraft.

While Mary was away at college, Laura studied seriously in the De Smet school. She felt it was her responsibility to become a teacher, both to please Ma and to help earn funds for Mary's college expenses. Laura's first job as a teacher came sooner than she expected.

In December of 1883, Laura had recited over half of the story of American history at a school exhibition in De Smet. A country school district heard about her work, and wanted Laura to teach there. Although she was not yet sixteen, which was then the legal age of a teacher, Laura passed the teacher's examination. No one asked about her age.

Laura's first teaching job was in an abandoned claim shanty twelve miles from De Smet. Laura was homesick so far from her family, and she felt timid when she first saw her six pupils. Two of them were older than she was! She lived with Mr. and Mrs. Bouchie, who semed to fight and complain from morning until night. Laura felt unwelcome, but was determined to earn the $40 promised her. She knew how much that money would help Pa, and she insisted on sticking out the two-month term of school.

As Laura's first week of teaching was ending, she was astonished to hear sleigh bells ringing outside the schoolhouse. It was Almanzo Wilder, a young homesteader from De Smet. He had driven his Morgan team and cutter across the prairie to take Laura back home for the weekend. She was relieved, but confused. Why would Almanzo offer her this kindness? She was often tongue-tied and bashful with him, and considered herself poor company. But she was so happy to be going home to Pa and Ma that she dismissed her class and scurried into the cutter.

Each Friday, Almanzo came for Laura and drove her back to her teaching duties on Sunday. Those were bitter drives and Laura often wondered why Almanzo bothered to travel over the snowy prairies. But joyfully, she rode behind the dashing team in the swift cutter. Once Laura told Almanzo bluntly that when school was over she would no longer ride with him.

But when Laura's teaching term ended and she was back in the De Smet school herself, Almanzo continued to appear at Pa's door, asking Laura to go riding. When spring came, Almanzo and Laura were often seen in his luxurious buggy. Girls were envious of Laura, and she found that Almanzo was good company as well as a good horseman.

Laura taught two more terms of school to earn money for Mary, but she never enjoyed teaching. Between her jobs, Laura rejoined her own class in De Smet, where the teacher, Ven Owen, was impressed with her work. Mr. Owen stressed writing skills and saw in Laura Ingalls a definite talent.   Laura had a wonderful mind, he told Pa, and should be given every chance for more education.

But Laura did not graduate from the De Smet school. At eighteen she had taught three terms of school. She felt she was a grown-up now, and she and Almanzo Wilder planned to be married.

Almanzo in his apple orchard (cover of the Ruralist, June 1, 1918).

Rocky Ridge Farm

□

*"I wished for an
artist's hand or a
poet's brain or even
to be able to tell in
good plain prose how
beautiful it was."*

Almanzo Wilder was ten years older than Laura. His life as a farmer boy in Malone, New York and in Spring Valley, Minnesota had prepared him to be a homesteader. In 1879, Almanzo had filed his claim for land near De Smet. But he homesteaded two 160-acre claims instead of the usual one. The second was a tree claim. The U.S. government allowed a settler a "tree claim" if he would plant and cultivate ten acres of saplings. On Almanzo's tree claim, the required acres of box elders, cottonwoods and elms were thriving when he started building a house for Laura. When the little house was completed, Almanzo painted it a soft gray. All around, trees grew, promising cool shade. In the fields beyond, Almanzo's crops sprouted up on the land he had broken with his sod plow.

Very quietly, on the morning of August 25, 1885, Laura and Almanzo drove to the Reverend Brown's house and were married. Laura, who was always independent and outspoken, asked for a change in the usual wedding ceremony. She objected to the use of the word "obey" in the wedding vows. "Even if I tried, I do not think I could obey anyone against my better judgement," she explained. Both Almanzo and Reverend Brown agreed. After a wedding dinner at home with Pa, Ma and Laura's sisters, they started life together on their farm a mile north of De Smet. "I was no longer a pioneer girl," Laura said, "but a homesteader's wife. And I had a house and home of my own."

Laura and Almanzo—Manly, Laura always called him— had a marriage which was unusual by Dakota standards in 1885. They decided to approach wheat farming as a partnership, consulting each other on every decision.

But the Wilders' attempts at wheat farming seemed doomed from the start for a drought cycle hit the Dakota prairie. "How heartbreaking it was," Laura remembered, "to watch the grain we had sown with such hope wither and yellow in the hot winds."

Their first four years of married life were full of hardships. Their only successful wheat crop was driven into the ground by hail. Fire destroyed the little gray house Manly had built.

Then diptheria nearly killed them both. Manly was left permanently weakened, and walked with a limp for the rest of his life. In the *The First Four Years*, which Laura did not publish during her lifetime, she wrote about those discouraging years.

During those hard years of homesteading, Laura became a mother. On a bitter prairie night, December 5, 1886, her only daughter was born. She was named Rose, for the masses of prairie roses which covered the prairie in June. Three years later, in August, 1889, Manly and Laura's only son was born. But like Laura's brother Freddie, he did not survive long. He lived only two weeks, and unnamed, was buried in the prairie sod of the De Smet Cemetery.

"No one who has not pioneered can understand the fascination and the terror of it," Laura said in summing up the rigors of her first years with Manly. But finally, the hardships became too great. To restore Manly's health, the young family left De Smet's searing hot summers and frigid winters.

Their first stop was a year-long visit with Almanzo's family in Spring Valley, Minnesota. Almanzo's family provided a comfort and shelter that Laura, Manly and Rose had not known during their years of disappointment and tragedy in South Dakota. But Manly still did not stop limping or regain his old vigor.

In 1891, they decided to go to Florida, where the warm climate might help Manly. There they settled in the village of Westville. "We went to live in the piney woods of Florida,"

Laura explained, "where the trees always murmur; where butterflies are enormous, where plants that eat insects grow in moist places and alligators inhabit the slowly moving waters of the rivers. But at that time and in that place a Yankee woman was more of a curiosity than any of these."

The Wilders stayed in Florida only a year; Laura could not endure the hot, muggy climate. Then they returned to De Smet again. In De Smet, the Wilders lived in a house in town, near the Ingalls home. Pa was a townsman now, operating a store, working as a carpenter and as a town official.

For two years, Manly and Laura worked to save money while Rose attended school. Laura sewed at the dressmaker's, sometimes twelve hours a day, for a dollar in wages. Manly found work when he could, but he was still not strong. Then, in 1894, Laura and Manly heard of "The Land of the Big Red Apple"—the Ozark country of Missouri. The Ozark country had a mild climate and was renowned for its fruit, poultry and dairy farming. The Wilders' decided to go there and it became Laura's final pioneering journey.

In July of 1894, the Wilders loaded all their possessions into a wagon and prepared to set out for their new home. Hidden in Laura's writing desk was a secret $100 bill. That was to be their money for a new start in Mansfield, Missouri. Pa and Ma, Mary, Carrie and Grace all stood around the house to see them off. Rose was seven, and she always remembered how blue her blind Aunt Mary's eyes were that summer morning.

As the Wilders headed south, Rose recalled how her mother kept a diary of the journey, writing in pencil in a nickel notebook.★

The Wilders traveled 650 miles through the drought-stricken states of South Dakota, Nebraska, and Kansas before they entered Missouri. They liked what they saw right away: Missouri was green and hilly. It looked covered with trees, after the burned, brown prairie. As the wagon creaked along the road through the Ozark hills, Laura was reminded of her long-ago life in the woods of Wisconsin. The Ozarks were really valleys, not mountains, and the ridge tops were level where they met the sky. Numberless springs tumbled out of the stony hillsides, and blackberries grew in the thickets. "There is no country in the world like the Ozarks," Laura declared.

On August 31, 1894, the Wilders arrived at their destination, a village called Mansfield. As the wagon rounded the bend into town, Laura said in a voice filled with hope: "This is where we stop."

It was. Manly and Laura looked over farms for sale in the region until they found what they wanted: a rough, rocky forty acres of land just a mile from the Mansfield town

★*Published as "On the Way Home"*

square. Laura immediately named the place Rocky Ridge Farm. The farm suited its name. Most of the land was uncleared. Flinty stones covered the gullies and sharp ridges. And at the top of one ridge stood the Wilders' new home: a leaky, windowless log cabin.

Laura made the cabin a cozy home, and saw that Rose was enrolled in the Mansfield school. At eight, Rose already showed signs of being a brilliant student who read everything she could lay her hands on.

Manly was still not strong, and Laura was his constant helper. "Our idea of an ideal home is one built by a man and woman together," Laura said. Rocky Ridge Farm was built that way. Laura helped her husband fell trees for firewood and building. Together, they planted the corn crop during the first spring, learned how to run an orchard and make the stubborn Ozark soil produce crops.

Life became easier on Rocky Ridge. The Wilders built a new house on a green knoll to replace the log cabin. When it was finished, the new farmhouse consisted of ten rooms of rustic nooks, a quaint open staircase, a library and a fine stone fireplace. As they added to the house, they increased the size of Rocky Ridge Farm until it consisted of 200 acres.

Laura became known for her successful poultry raising. People were curious to learn how she could clear a dollar profit per hen. "She gets eggs in winter when none of her neighbors get eggs," said one Ozark neighbor with admiration. Laura said her methods were simple, and was often asked to appear at farmer's meetings to share her ideas.

Once when Laura was asked to present a talk she was too busy helping Manly at home. She sent her speech ahead to be read in her absence. In the audience that day was an editor from the farm family weekly, *The Missouri Ruralist*. He was so impressed by Laura's arrangement of words that he offered her the job of household editor for the *Ruralist*.

Laura eagerly accepted the job. Between her farm chores and housework, she somehow found time to write a steady stream of poetry, articles, interviews and essays for the *Ruralist*. Her first article appeared in February, 1911; Laura had just turned 44. In most of her *Missouri Ruralist* columns, Laura wrote about country life and her own experiences on Rocky Ridge Farm. Her writing showed how truly content she was with life on a farm. Laura wrote: "A moment's pause to watch the glory of a sunrise or a sunset is soul-satisfying, while a bird's song will set the steps to music all day long."

Rose Wilder (Laura's daughter) in graduation dress.

Mother and Daughter

□

*"Your log cabin in the
Great Woods...your
trip through Kansas
...the building of
the railroad through
the Dakotas...Make
it real, because you
saw it with your
own eyes."*

While Manly and Laura were firmly rooted to life in the Ozark country, Rose, by contrast, was eager to see the world beyond the Missouri hills. At sixteen she went to live with Manly's sister, Eliza Jane, in Crowley, Louisiana to attend high school. In her single year of school in Crowley, Rose learned the four years of Latin required to graduate.

Rose also learned telegraphy at the little railroad station in Mansfield. By the time she turned seventeen, she was working for Western Union in Kansas City. She was one of the "bachelor girls," famous for wearing a modified man's shirt, shorter skirt and bobbed hair.

Laura observed thousands of girls like her own Rose struggling for what they called "women's rights". But she had never felt restricted by her own life as a farm woman. "We who live in quiet places," Laura remarked, "have the opportunity to become acquainted with ourselves, to think our own thoughts and live our own lives."

Laura agreed with her daughter that women should lead independent lives, but she had never felt that her role on Rocky Ridge Farm had been anything but an equal partnership with Almanzo. "Farm women have always been businesswomen and no one has even noticed it," she mentioned in one of her columns. Laura favored a practical, useful role for women on the farm and in business, and she was intolerant of situations in which females were not treated with respect.

By 1908, Rose was working in San Francisco and a short while later she married Gillette Lane. Soon she became one of the first women to sell real estate in California. Rose sold farmland in the Bay area until she was asked to work as a writer for the *San Farancisco Bulletin* several years later. Within a short time, Rose Wilder Lane had become a well-known celebrity journalist. In 1915, Rose persuaded Laura to leave Rocky Ridge for a long vacation in San Francisco.

Laura was eager to visit Rose and see all the sights. But she also wished to confer with Rose about writing. She saw how successful her daughter had become in a short time. She wanted her advice about her own writing career. "I am hoping to do some writing that will count," Laura confided to Manly. She wrote him regularly, describing all the sights she visited, particularly the 1915 World's Fair. She also told of the discussions she and Rose had about the writing profession.

But when she returned to Rocky Ridge, Laura once again became too involved with life on the farm to pursue writing more seriously. She took on a new project, the establishment of a farm loan company. By founding the Mansfield Farm Loan Association, the Wilders and their neighbors could borrow money at low interest rates. Laura became the first secretary-treasurer of the loan company which was a local branch of the Federal Loan Bank.

Cheerfully, Laura doled out over a million dollars of government money in small loans to her Ozark neighbors. She managed the business from after World War I into the 1920's. During this time, there was never a delayed payment or an unpaid loan. Laura used her small corner study off the bedroom in Rocky Ridge Famhouse as her office. There she met loan applicants and kept careful records of the business.

There too, she continued to write her columns for the *Ruralist*.

Laura's work was well-known in the Ozarks, but Rose's writings were achieving national attention. In 1917, she wrote *Henry Ford's Own Story*, the first biography of the auto magnate. Her first novel, *Diverging Roads*, was the story of a country girl in the big city, her marriage and divorce.

While Laura's life followed a peaceful routine, Rose's life was beginning to grow hectic. Following her divorce in 1918, Rose accepted a job in Europe with the American Red Cross. She was assigned to write about the conditions of refugees and orphans in the aftermath of World War I. Rose stayed abroad four years, adding many articles, short stories and books to her list of published works.

Rose's success as a writer made Laura and Manly very proud. But her long absences from home interfered with a growing writing relationship with her mother.

Nevertheless, it was Rose who got Laura to submit an article on farm life to *McCall's*. "Here is your chance to make a real income!" she told her mother. "Sidetrack anything that can be sidetracked...there is no reason why you should not be making four or five thousand a year writing."

In 1924, Rose returned to America and settled on Rocky Ridge Farm. She modernized the old family farmhouse and built a new modern cottage for Laura and Almanzo nearby. In her upstairs writing porch, Rose wrote magazine serials, two Ozark novels, titled *Hill-Billy* and *Cindy*, and published a steady stream of short stories and articles.

Laura watched all of Rose's literary activities with interest. She had turned sixty in 1927, and had given up her loan company work. She seldom even wrote for the *Ruralist* anymore. But Rose would not allow Laura to settle into a quiet old age. She encouraged her mother to write her autobiography.

Laura decided to try. On blue-lined tablets, with a soft-lead pencil, Laura wrote her life story from her Big Woods childhood to her 1885 wedding. The manuscript was called "Pioneer Girl." Rose typed the manuscript and sent it to her agent in New York City. Nothing happened. Editors said there were too many older Americans writing about their lives during pioneer times.

But Rose and Laura were not discouraged. Instead, Laura decided to write a children's book, featuring many of the tales Pa had told in the "little houses." "These were family stories and I believed they should be preserved," Laura said. So she gathered her memories of life in the Big Woods of Wisconsin and wrote *Little House in the Big Woods*. Harper and Brothers published the book in 1932, when Laura was sixty-five. It was an immediate success.

Laura and Rose on the Rocky Ridge Farm.

Pioneer Author

□

> *"I understood that
> in my own life I
> represented a period of
> American History."*

Laura was surprised at the success of her first book. "I thought that would end it," she said. "But what do you think? Children who read it wrote to me begging for more. I was amazed, because I didn't know how to write!"

With her publisher and Rose both encouraging her, Laura wrote her second book, *Farmer Boy*, which was published in 1933. *Farmer Boy* was the story of Almanzo's boyhood on a big farm in upstate New York during the 1860's. "I am not much of a hand to tell a story, much less write it," Almanzo admitted, but he patiently told Laura about his childhood, the farm, and the people and places he remembered.

Laura's third book, *Little House on the Prairie*, appeared in 1935. By this time, her plan for a multi-volume saga of her pioneer memories was fully accepted by Harper and Brothers, who eagerly awaited each complete book. So did Laura's new family of reader-friends.

Each day, when Manly brought in the mail, there were handfuls of letters to Laura from her readers. Children, parents, teachers and librarians all wrote her, wanting to know what happened next to the Ingalls family. These readers begged for more books, telling her how much they enjoyed her stories. Laura was reminded of the way Rose used to beg, "Please tell me just one more story!"

So Laura continued penciling her stories in the five-cent "Fifty-Fifty" school tablets which she bought at the local grocery store. In 1937, she published *On the Banks of Plum Creek* and planned the rest of her "Little House" books which would all have their setting in the Dakota Territory.

Rose worked closely with Laura on all the "Little House" books, but eventually she left Rocky Ridge to live and write in New York. Her own books about the homesteading days, *Let the Hurricane Roar* and *Free Land* became famous bestsellers. But she still found time to be her mother's adviser. "What you write is always good," Rose assured Laura, who sometimes became discouraged.

Before Laura wrote her Dakota books, she and Manly went back to De Smet to visit. In 1938, and again in 1939, they drove all the way to South Dakota in their Chrysler. "Everywhere we went we recognized faces" Laura said, "but we were always surprised to find them old and gray like

Laura, at the time she was writing for The Missouri Ruralist.

ourselves, instead of being young as in our memories."

Laura checked details of history in De Smet, asked questions of old-timers, and refreshed her memories. And she and Manly visited Laura's sisters. Pa, Ma and Mary were dead, but Carrie and Grace still lived in South Dakota. Grace was now Mrs. Nate Dow and she lived in Manchester. Carrie was Mrs. David Swanzey. She lived at the foot of Mount Rushmore in the Black Hills. Laura and Manly stopped there to see the massive faces of Washington, Jefferson, Lincoln and Roosevelt which were being carved on the granite mountainside.

Laura's last books were completed in quick succession. In 1939, *By the Shores of Silver Lake* was published, followed by *The Long Winter* in 1940. In 1941, *Little Town on the Prairie* was completed. When *These Happy Golden Years* appeared in 1943, Laura was seventy-six. *Golden Years* concluded with her marriage to Almanzo. It was the end of the "Little House" stories.

Laura's eleven-year writing stint on the "Little House" books was the richest harvest of her long life. Together, her books had created a complete, vivid picture of American pioneer living, and their popularity grew greater each year. The thousands of letters she received, the honors, tributes and awards, were an unexpected joy in Laura's old age. But despite this she remained the same modest, quiet person she had always been. Most people in Mansfield thought of her as the lady from Rocky Ridge who walked into town with a basket of eggs over her arm to trade, not as a famous author. Laura was comfortable with that image, but deeply pleased at the fact that her stories would not be forgotten.

Manly and Laura seldom stirred from Rocky Ridge. They went to town each Wednesday; they took drives, winding through the Ozark hills; in the evenings they read and listened to the radio. Almanzo tinkered in his workshop and tended his goat herd, while Laura kept house and answered her fan mail. It was not unusual for the mailbox to be stuffed with fifty letters a day from Laura's admirers. In her careful longhand, on the same lined paper she had used to write her books, Laura answered each one.

Many of the letters asked hopefully if the "Little House" books were true stories. Laura replied to a class of fourth graders: "You ask if Laura was a real person. She was. I am the Laura you have been reading about, grown up now."

She was also happy to tell her readers that she had lived everything she had written in her books. "The books are true stories, written from Almanzo's and my own memories." But Laura admitted that since the pioneer days, "times have changed indeed within my memory...As I remember things of which I told in my stories, I can hardly believe I was the same person as the Laura of whom I wrote."

The companionable years with Manly on Rocky Ridge continued through the 1940s. But on October 23, 1949, Almanzo died suddenly at Rocky Ridge. He was nearly 93. The Wilders had been married sixty-four years.

After her husband's death, Laura continued to live alone on the farm, but was never lonely. Flashes of the old pioneer girl sparked when her friends and her daughter Rose objected to her living alone. "I have a shotgun and a pistol and I know how to use them!" Laura sputtered.

But all her visitors were friendly ones. Rose made visits from her home in Danbury, Connecticut, and friends from Mansfield often called. Each summer, cars arrived at Rocky Ridge, hoping to meet Laura. She was always generous to her readers, inviting them to tour the old house, or chatting on the porch swing. Laura joked that she thought tourists much outdo farmers in early rising; one family arrived at her door at seven in the morning!

Along with her fan mail came news of increasing recognition for the "Little House" books. Laura was pleased when the United States State Department ordered her books translated into German and Japanese because they were positive representations of America. That brought Laura a new audience and mail from abroad. Eventually her books were translated into over fifty languages.

On her eighty-fourth birthday in 1951, 900 greetings arrived at Rocky Ridge, along with cakes and gifts from many states. Libraries were named for Laura in Detroit, Michigan, Pomona, California, and in Mansfield just down the road from Rocky Ridge. "It is hard for me to believe all this honor has come to me," Laura admitted. When the Laura Ingalls Wilder Award was established by the American Library Association in 1954 (and the first medal presented to Laura herself), she said: "When writing down those memories of my long-ago childhood, I had no idea they would be so well received, and it is a continual delight to me that they should be so well-loved."

Part of Laura's satisfaction in her books' success came from her belief in the importance of American principles and independence in the pioneer era she wrote about. "I sometimes have a homesick longing for the old days and the old ways," she confessed.

Of all the modern progress Laura saw in America, she was not entirely approving. She said:

It seems impossible to me that I have seen so many changes in living, some very good, some very wrong in my opinion. The old spirit of sturdy independence seems to be vanishing. We all depend too much on others. As modern life is lived, we have to do so, and more and more the individual alone is helpless. A conflict with nature and the elements is a clean fight, but a struggle against man and his contrivances is something very different. At

times I have a homesick longing, but there is no turning back.
We must go on...

Laura's life marched on. She accepted each tribute to her work with pleasure, and watched the world outside of Rocky Ridge with interest. She so wanted to reach the milestone of her ninetieth birthday, because Almanzo had. And she did. On February 7, 1957, the house on Rocky Ridge was full of cards, presents, cakes and tributes to the grand lady who had written the "Little House" books. Rose was visiting to help make Laura's 90th birthday especially memorable.

Laura lived three days after her birthday, dying at home on February 10, 1957. Her readers in schools, libraries and little houses all over the world mourned her, but somehow people knew that Laura would always remain real and near through her books.

Though her frontier life was of the long-ago past, Laura Ingalls Wilder's faith in the future was unflinching. This was clear when she wrote that:

Many things have changed since I beat eggs with a fork or cleaned a kerosene lamp. But the truths we learned from our parents and the principles they taught us are always true; they can never change. Great improvements in living have been made because every American has been able to pursue his happiness, and so long as Americans are free they will continue to make our country ever more wonderful.

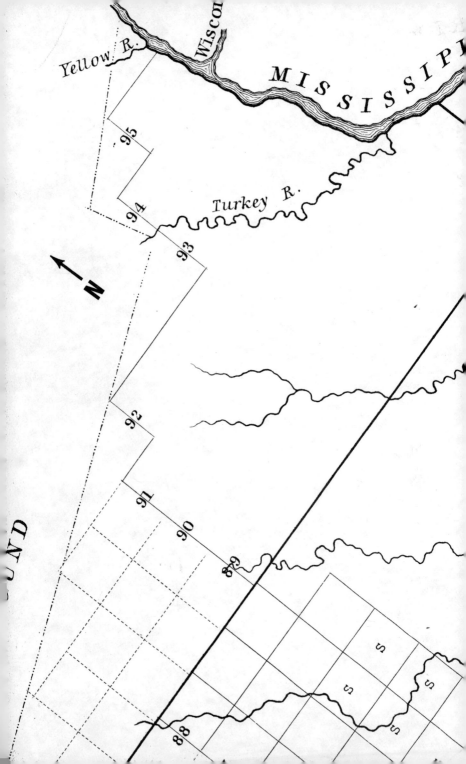